STEP INTO MY VISIONS

STEP INTO MY VISIONS

IDLE THOUGHTS IN POETRY

God Bless you Lisa
"ENJOY"
love from
Barbara Hewitt.
x

D.K. BABACH

Print information available on the last page.

Rev. date: 04/06/2020

To order additional copies of this book, contact:
Xlibris
800-056-3182
www.Xlibrispublishing.co.uk
Orders@Xlibrispublishing.co.uk
810301

Contents

Some Storm!

From across the ocean comes the breeze
I love the smell but it makes me sneeze
The clouds are dull with a grey overtone
I suppose it's to do with the - 'Ozone.'
Now comes the rain though quite mild
But it won't be long before the sea runs wild.
It comes from the North, this bad weather
And the gulls seem to float as light as a feather.

The wind is picking up soon to be a gale
And it's so amazing to watch the seagulls sail
They grow quite noisy as the tide comes in
I love the sounds as the waves begin
By now the rain begins to pour and I am getting wet
But it does not really worry me, or at least, not yet
I feel I want to stay a while so as to understand
The pressure that's absorbed by the beaches golden sand

The sea comes in as though alive, its force is very grand
As waves now crash against the rocks, I can touch it with my hand
The spray like clouds forming anew, are seen with such delight
As all the rainbow colours seem to glow amid the light.
I love the storm with all its strength and all its mighty power
But it now proves too much for me. 'I'll return to Blackpool
Tower.'

The Face

The face we know can tell a lot
From the eyes that look at you
They can sparkle they can respond
They can be brown, green or blue

They can change in an instant
Depends on what they see
When they are happy
They will dance with glee

When they are sad
A frown will appear
And when there is pain
They may shed a tear

When deep in thought the eyes will glaze
Especially when in love
You see the mouth it will also react
In tune with the eyes above

A droopy mouth means you are sad
Maybe about to cry
A cheery grin means you are glad
(If you had wings then you could fly)

A gaping mouth with a deep breath
Along with eyes like saucers
Often means you have a sight
Of something that is nauseous

Lips held tight means you maybe
Trying to control some anger
Because some words have come out
And you may have dropped a clanger

I for one will give God praise
For you 'always being there'
The special face is one that shows
That you do really care.!

Colour

Colour is a useful word
There are so many colours
Colours that are all around
In everything it covers.

Colours that surround us
Both outside and in the home
At the seaside in the woods
Wherever we do roam

Now let us see as we think
Of colour's on this earth.
So much our eyes can see
In our lives from our birth.

A baby's eyes that focus
On the eyes of its new mother
Then there are the eyes
Of father, sister, brother.

Then to see the baby smile
As its vision is unfurled.
The colours that surround
The babies little world

The child may then come across
Someone's family pet
A black cat, a brown dog
And so many never met.

And as the child develops
It wonders at the view
Like a goldfish, blue budgie
Green frog, to name a few

Now this child be a boy or girl
Hair blonde, brown or black
Hair could be even red
With curls at the back

Sitting in its buggy,
It is taken for a walk
It is so fascinated,
And now begins to talk

Of the green grass the tall trees
The people as they pass
Their coloured coats, shoes and hats
Are reflected in the glass

To see the swings and roundabouts
Coloured blue and yellow
With many children running round
And hearing parents bellow!

White fluffy clouds adorn the sky
Amid the brightest blue
With lots of birds that made the child
Excited when they flew

I am that child with God's gift
Of colours to be found
And I apply the colours
To my verses when they sound

Sometimes full of beauty
Warm and often sunny
Some can be of abstract
Colourful and funny

But the greatest colour of them all
I must say before we part
Is that of Our Father's love that
God has planted in my heart.
Amen

Sunshine fruit has gone with the Summer

Five fruit and veg 'is a must they say'
With summer gone we have the Autumn fare.
With beans, carrots, and fruit, 'it must be 5 a day.'
Whether it be apple, banana, peach or pear.

Now October is here, it is harvest time
But still we rely on imported crops
With strange names of fruit and veg,
The advice on our nutrition never stops.

Not just the '5 a day,' the experts tell
But all manner of food is a target.
With the process foods with additives
The worse place is the 'supermarket.

Prepared meals, although the are handy
Our Grandmothers knew what was best
Homemade pies, cakes and stew
Try putting it all to the test.

Fresh fish, meat, fresh bread
The market is the place to be.
All kinds of fresh fruit galore
The choice is there to see

To watch my mother on baking day
Was always a great pleasure
Her dumpling stew and her pastries
She really was a treasure

But no '5 a day' in days of old
Most times the food was good
No thoughts of fruit or fibre
'Food like that?' if only we could.!

Good thing I love 'fruit and Veg!

Where has our summer gone?

Here it is 2009 as we wonder?
"Where has the summer gone"?
It is now near the end of August
And the sun has hardly ever shone!

All hopes were dashed more than once
When we wanted to arrange 'a get together'
When having planned a garden party
It was 'ruined' by 'bad weather.'

Not knowing what to wear
With confusion and even doubt
We take a sun hat and umbrella
whenever we venture out

It maybe sunny in the morning
And change to rain in the afternoon
Turning what was to be a bright day
Into a more depressing 'gloom'

It is raining really hard in the morning
You may have to go to the shop
After getting really soaking wet
You get home and the rain will stop!

You put some washing on the line
Trusting the weather again
You wait until its almost dry
When down comes the pouring rain!

What has happened to the weather?
Many plans have gone astray
I for one will stay indoors
Well that's my forecast for today.

My Flat Pack

Have you ever had a "flat pack"
Maybe a wardrobe or a bed?
Well now "I've" got one
A "metal" garden shed!

I am looking forward to seeing
The shed when complete
But on seeing the kit needed
The instructions have me beat.

Two people are needed
It says so on the pack
To put the shed together
"What with MY bad back"!

I will have to see what I can do
To get hold of two strong men
I not only have to think of 'how'
But also think of 'when'

It's true I need it yesterday
As I need a real safe place
So instead of a wooden shed
It's one anchored at the base

As I need a little scooter
The mobility kind
And having a safe 'lock up'
Is the rule, I find

So here's hoping it won't be long
Before I can get about
But seeing this big 'flat pack'
My saying 'soon' is really - in doubt.
Oh well.....

I fancied a ride

I have a bus pass and I fancied a ride
'Where to' at the bus stop, I had to decide.
I ask myself, 'why today?' I still ponder yet
I must have been mad since the day was wet.
Used to driving my car, whatever the weather
I have not used a bus for what seems forever.

I looked at the numbers to see where they go.
I felt that I wanted someplace I know
I did not want to use a bus that went very far
But just a little further than I'd been in the car.
I could go Leek or I could go to Crewe
At least these were places that I knew

But then there was Congleton I could visit my friend
But I took a bus to Longton 'to shop' in the end.
I should have been adventurous but maybe next time
I'll make much better use, of this bus pass of mine.
Still I enjoyed seeing people come on board
And glad to be dry, when the rain really poured.

The trip on the bus has made me think even more
To try and go to places that, I've NOT been before.
There is no pressure I can take my time
To travel on my own, is just fine.
It just remains for me, to put my bus pass away
In a safe place 'til, an 'adventurous' day.

Our Church and the Ash Bank

To Rev. John and the church we really must thank
For the meal that we enjoyed at The Ash Bank
For Trevor and his crew, it all went so well
As the Elderberries here are so keen to tell

The transport provided got us there on time
Even the weather had stayed fine
There was Minnie in her wheelchair
(not liking it one bit)
She insisted that, on a 'real chair' she'd rather sit

Four of our ladies were waited on
At the table that they were to dine
Most of us went to get our lunch
Well, we were in our prime!

Drinks were served with compliments
This really was a treat
Our plates were full of veggies
And three kinds of meat

Following the lovely meal
There was coffee or a pot of tea
And what made it all so special
Was that it was all Free!

Now a week later we can all reflect
On what God provided that day
The Elderberries should now elect
Trevor, 'we're here to Stay.'

Amen!!

The Blue Fragrance

The wonderful fragrance in the air
The hydrangea, lavender, hyacinth, too
I'd picked many bluebells from under the trees
The great mass was quite a view.

The forget - me - not so dainty and of a delicate blue
Written on love letters, that were maybe sent to you.
So too the tiny pansy that seem to dance so bright
Among the blue labella they look so sweet, just right.

Today I heard a peacock so loud and so pure
I then saw him strutting like he never strut before
I was struck by the vivid blue so rich and colorful
From his head to his draping tail it was so beautiful.

There goes that noise again as he begins his display
Because a rather dull peahen, has just come by his way.
This very proud peacock did not fail to amaze
In showing us his feathers and his very special ways.

While the bees are loudly buzzing around their hive
The brightest of sunshine has brought the blues alive.
A day with such beauty still can still be found
Adding to the fragrance that is all around.

The blue of the butterfly and the little blue bird
Brings my day to a close with this final word
I've enjoyed my blue vision, my interesting day
But I really must leave now and be on my way.

Feet

Do you ever "think" about your feet!
The miles they cover, when on the beat.

When they are icy cold, or maybe stink
When they give you pain and you have to think!

Where to put them and wish they could talk
What would they say, as you take that walk?

I would like mine to say, that they would stay warm
And even get rid of my painful corn.

My feet are not dainty like some I see
They're a big "clobb hopper" below each knee!

To get big shoes is not a delight
The style alone is never right.

Slippers, sandals, boots or shoe
They hurt the most when they are new!

I soak my feet most every day
This does take some of the pain away.

These feet of mine are truly blessed
I mean, they are "the very best".

Modes of transport here today
So with all their faults,
"They are here to stay"!

How stupid is this ode to feet.....
"No worse than London's "plates of meat!!'

My toe did not behave!

I have a toe that was deformed
Not a pretty sight
I had an operation
And I thought I'd put it right
The operation did the job
And for a while looked good
But the toe did not behave
'Cos it should have understood.
But no, and what's even worse
It got the next toe to join in
But I don't think that this toe
Knew it would end up with a pin.
So today I've paid the price
The toe's had it's it revenge
Pins in place they look just like
Stones, standing at Stonehenge.
My poor foot is hurting
With **two** pins in this time,
But I should think, by Christmas
That my toes should be quite fine
The thing that I miss the most
Is driving my little car
Because without my driving
I cannot go very far.

So here I am with crutches
Having stitches taken out
Relying on special people
So that I can get about.
I could so easily stay at home
With my foot up in the air
Then get into an awful rut
By staying in my chair
But then I'd miss my friends.
The ones I see today
So I will sit among you
Now that I've had my say

Thank you...

A Book Addict

I have a friend who loves to read.
Reads many, many books indeed
At the library you may see my friend
Choosing 6 or 7 books to lend.
She spends most times in her bed
Reading until her books are read.
I often wonder why I don't look
And choose to read a real nice book.
But my interest is at this time
To write this poetry (and more) in rhyme.
I am often asked how do I cope
As the world out there has so much scope.
But I am happy to use my head,
Using many visions instead.
I have a new vision almost every day
But this vision of my friend
Will do for today.

Thank you.

I Saw Something Move

I was in the kitchen, arms in the sink
When I saw something move in a flash
Not knowing what I'd find
I looked in every room
If I saw something move, I would dash
I must be really careful
I mustn't charge around
Then again I may not see it,
It may have gone to ground...
But I saw this white rabbit
Being pulled by a string
There was my young son
Dressed up like a king
Thankfully the rabbit
Was just a toy
My fear then turned to love
For this mischievous little boy
'Ah, bless him'

Those Special Tiny Babies

I have today began to knit
Something small to start
Like really tiny bonnets
For babies close to my heart.

The tiny babies that fight for life
No bigger than a kitten
Needing so much special care
The kind that can't be written.

Dedicated nurses that take care
Support the parents too
Most of these tiny babies
Arrive before they're due.

I am sure that God gives the skills
To doctors that attend
These very special babies
To be with them 'till the end.

Surrounded by their family
With so much love to give.
A lot of these tiny babies
Win the fight to live.

So I will keep on knitting
With the softest baby wool
For these very special babies
Because they're wonderful.

Amen

My Own Little Chap

"What are you doing"? As I enter the room
"Mind the plant - stop chasing that balloon!"
I know you are overactive but this is outrageous
Your enthusiastic pressure can be very dangerous

(I must be very sensitive and answer him with care)
When trying to have a conversation and knowing just where
It will lead to, as I don't think he'll say sorry
But IF he responds WELL, I will return his lorry.

He has always been a handful, this little chap of mine
Once again my back is turned - He's like this all the time!
I wonder where his energy is stored up every day?
I'd like to grab hold of it, and throw some of it away.

But then he would no longer be this energetic chap
He would always be here, laying on my lap
I would get nothing done or worry myself sick
So I will just have to watch while a football he will kick.

He loves to play "goal" in the garden, using the back gate
It is always fun to watch him with his little mate
It's pouring down with rain, outside today
So it's inside the house, where he has to play

Oh well another day to get through
Busy as ever with his baby sister too
I just have to be patient, I WILL get some rest
When daddy puts them to bed, "ah that's the best"

Wait a minute, what's this little heap?
Oh bless the little chap, he is fast asleep.
I love this little chap, asleep or awake
But I also love the chance like this
To have a "well earned break!"

I love my Job

I love my job and my mates
And even my Boss too
But I cannot face being late
And often wonder what to do.
Imagine the clock radio
Was silent when switched on
You believe it must be broken
And wonder where time has gone
Your Boss will not believe you
You don't believe it yourself
I know I get quite nervy
And wish I had poor health
'Cos I would do 'a sicky'
And do my best somehow
To make sure that my clock radio
Was always working now

Wow a week has gone
And I've not been late
My clock radio is working well
So this weekend me and my mates

Will meet by the cottage
Named "Bluebell"
We plan to go shopping
at the garden centre in Leigh
Then later we'll have a Bar Be Que
Just in time for tea.

At the garden centre
We had a look around
Then went to the café
To discuss what we had found
Some cages in the corner
Had some birds that flew about
There was also a Miner Bird
That could talk, there was no doubt.
The rabbits and the guinea pigs
Were very cute indeed
A notice was close by
Telling people "do not feed"
Then there were plants for the garden
Of every kind and shape
And the ponds were protected
By some bright yellow tape.

Two of my mates were laden
With their goods placed in a pack
And in no time at all
It was time to go back.
We headed for the car parked
A few yards away
And then finished with the Bar Be Que
At the end of the day.

At the Pavillian

This place is one in a million
Having never seen this pavilion
I am here with a crowd
Under a black cloud
But having a laugh
Along the winding path
Leading to a tea room
Where we shall soon
Along with some fun
Have some tea and a bun

We've been having a race
All over the place
(Having tripped on a wedge
I fell into a hedge)
Though pleased with what we've just done
Nobody, had really won
Still never mind as we relax and sit
With a couple of us "full of wit"
We are all happy no matter what
As we discuss just how far, we each have got

You see we all suffer with mental health
And we help each other out
So this trip to this pavilion
Is what it's all about.
We are surrounded by the gardens
But at this time of year
The flowers and their foliage
Are yet to still appear.
We shall come back in the summer
And sit outside and have our tea
With the gardens looking wonderful
What a great day that will be.

My Comp

I love my computer and using the mouse
It gives me brain food when in the house.
When it comes to life it makes me think
A click on the mouse makes the pointer wink.
It seems to wait patiently until I decide
What I want to do next as the options are wide
The choice normally depends on how I feel
I am often surprised at what I reveal
I may choose a game on MSN
I have already tried about ten
I enjoy the card games and matching up three
Of many kind of items that amuses me.
I also like to venture on the internet explorer
When I see what I like I save it in the file storer
I also like the contact I have with my friends
There are some lovely emails that my friend sends
This friend is a Christian and lives in Brazil
She has always been a blessing and always will.
I also use the computer to seek and find
Ideas in creating many cards of any kind.

I am able to print many documents fancy or plain
Until I run out of ink then it is a pain.
Once a week I sit brain dead in front of the screen
Steam coming from my ears, you know what I mean.
I want to create a poem with a rhyming verse
It can sometimes be easy and sometimes a curse
But here I am again to God I did pray
And so with God's help this is my poem for you today.

Thank you.

My Dad and Time

I was shown some photographs
Of an ocean liner
Of when my dad retired
He was a coal miner
Both mum and dad had been abroad
Touring many places while aboard
My poor dad no longer with us
Loved us all to bits
He had worked very hard
While working down the pits.
I can still remember
He'd come home for tea
He would give a welcome cuddle
Leaving coal dust over me.
However mum put up with it
All those years ago
But then she took great care of dad
Of that I really know
In due course the pits all closed
And changed our way of life
So 'just living' was much harder
And caused a lot of strife.

Thankfully the 60's came
'Then' we saw the light!
Although we were restricted
By a curfew every night.
'What a change'!
Just the fashion alone
Teddy boys, flared skirts
And winkle picker that we'd own.
The birth of the 'Teenager'
No longer needed to enlist
This gave a lot of freedom
But with a dreadful twist
Life has changed so very much
The race is really on
I know it must sound awful,
but I am glad my dad has gone.
But still I must move forward
As in this world I am
Trying to keep up
I really hope I can
The phase of fashion
has long gone by
As the there is no limit
In what the kids will try.
They do not seem to have the will
To have the respect we had
All of those many years ago
When we had our mum and dad.

But my poor mum, now senile
Cannot recall the days
Of when she was so special
In all of her loving ways.
It really is a worry
And it is really sad
That mum will never know
How I miss the love we had
As now I sit here with her
And say my last my goodbye
I thank God for mum and dad
As It's my turn now to try
And be the loving parent
So that when I leave this place
My family will know we have
Lived by God's Grace.

Little Lost Piano

I saw this piano last Tuesday afternoon
It looked a little lost In the corner of the room
I was visiting a friend While her husband was away
It had been a bad morning so I decided to stay
I lacked the energy To do much else you see
But a strong cup of coffee Should revive me
I love to indulge in The banana cake with cream
That this friend of mine Produces like in a dream
She had also knit a jumper That I love with a passion
This helps me so much To keep up with the fashion
I asked who plays the piano She said her husband did
But that he is away so much She would love it to be rid
We would chat away together Then the time would appear
To say my visits over, loud and clear
So I got my coat and My handbag too
On reaching the door I said "thank you"
My friend has promised That when we next meet
We will visit her friend Who lives further down the street.
She also bakes a splendid" Tasty shepherds pie."
"I look forward to it, yes," Then I said goodbye.

I thought about that piano And wish that I could play
I could ask my friend to teach me, I wonder what she'd say
But then her husband is the pianist so that is no use
I will just have to forget it but that is no excuse
Because that little lost piano is just asking to be played
In that lonely old corner where it has always stayed
I wish it lived in my house I am sure that it would fit
Of course! MY husband plays now I think of it
The thought of this has bugged me so much so
That I rang my friend asking if she would let it go.
I told her how I was feeling and the reason why
Then after some debating, I at last got a reply
The lonely little piano is no longer looking drab
It is now with me and is looking really FAB.
I have asked my husband to teach me how to play
I am now so pleased as he said "Yes one day"

My son is a policeman

As I instruct my son 'a police man' to shut the garden gate
I also check on Solo always hoping I'm not too late.
Solo is our pet mongrel who likes to sleep all day in her basket
She will only raise her sleepy head whenever we walk past it.
But just about two weeks ago she gave us all a fright
We found her basket empty due to an oversight.
I thought that the gate was closed so did my husband Jim
Later we realized when my son left our Solo had followed him.

So here I am in the living room relaxing before I bake
One of our favorite sponges, an upside down, rhubarb cake.

My husband has gone for a plant at the Castle Road garden centre
I do not like to go with him as he is known as "the tormenter"
Don't get me wrong he is a lovely man as gentle as can be
But he really is a pain whenever he torments me.
He is really solid and may I say he's tough
Trouble is when playful he can be really rough!
My son is "a chip off the old block" and can take it on the chin
I am not surprised he's a policeman, I am so proud of him.

My dad has been a policeman He is still a wonderful guy
He has now retired but I often wondered why.

He did not want to talk of it but my son and he are close
When at last my dad confided about the time it hurt the most.
Dad had been present at an incident where a family had been shot
He was also injured by this bloke who was high on POT.
The outcome had been bad, he had not thought about himself
Only the family that had died leaving dad safe but in poor health.
I am glad the he has told his story maybe now he can move on
Ah, here is Jim with an orchid, I forgot he'd even gone.

Now we are fed and watered we lounge on our settee
We have the usual cuddle and watch our wide screen TV.

'Til next time. 'Bye

True Happiness

I really know "true happiness",
'Though it comes in many forms.
It proves to be the strongest
After many storms

I sometimes find what lies ahead
Can be beyond control
A storm for me can be so bad
It can drive me "up the pole"!

Between the storms I have to grip
Onto the situation
Praying that my faith will hold
'Til the victory gives "elation"!

Then my freedom can compare
With the mighty eagle
Souring with the greatest ease
So high it looks so regal.

Happiness brings with it
Real love and true compassion
Believing that the spirit inside
Is giving me "full ration".

People see me happy
And wonder how I cope
I tell them of my great faith
That gives me so much hope.

I cannot always understand
Why there is sometimes so much pain
I guess it is to test my faith
In my lifetime to sustain.

Many times when feeling low
I do my very best
To let my spirit lift me up
Then I know I am truly blessed.

My Father God is at work
For ever and a day
He knows what lies ahead for me
And wants me to honour him and pray.

Jesus is my roll model
I love him through and through
It makes me feel so safe inside
And I know he loves me too.

Though I am a sinner
My forgiveness is so real
Having Jesus as my Savior
Means my sorrows he can heal.

Today I wondered what this verse
Would really be about
Then my dear granddaughter
Said "happiness" without a doubt.

So I will end this message
And share this love with you
While wishing you all much happiness
With many blessings too.

Thank you.

A Shock on the Rock

My friends and I went on a trip
To see an old, pirate ship
As we went to inspect
Around the lower deck
We asked "what was the matter"
Each one looking 'puzzled'
As there was a load of clatter!

The situation was very strange
They were searching for the banner
I asked though feeling very shy
If they needed this large spanner

But at last to everyone's relief
And from out of the blue
Someone had come aboard
Offering to come to the rescue

After some time the banner was found
It was unfurled as it began to rise
No wonder it had been lying around
Because of it's enormous size!

We all left before the banner was shown
We needed to leave them to it
We, by now had other plans
To climb some rocks to the summit.

So in climbing boots and having our packs
We then begin to climb
Hoping that the weather holds
Because right now its fine

Since I have never climbed before
I was not sure of my footing
Believe me, I wasn't sure
Of what danger I was putting

I saw the summit and its height
I only hoped I'd do it right
But when less, than half the way
I was breathless, I began to sway

I looked around hoping to find
That someone had seen me losing my mind
I try to hold on the best way I can
I begin to think that I should have ran

All at once all my friends could see
And they became afraid for me

I begin to panic and freeze on the spot
Not knowing just where to turn
I know that I could lose my grip
Giving me great concern

I really must take hold of myself
As help is on its way
I really wish that I had known best
Than to try to climb today

Well here I am at last on the terra firma
It is back to the drawing board
Because I'm still a learner
I wait until my friends return
With all the tales they tell
But mostly of the shock
Had I ever slipped and fell

I tell them I am sorry
but that they have all done well
In getting me down from the rocks
Then blushing I admit
I deserve to be put in the stocks!

THE END

The Rhyme

I feel I need to take the time
To work out something to do with rhyme
First I think of the American dime
Leading me to think of their gold mine.
I think of the grapes that grow on the vine
Of when they are used to produce wine.
I like the way that dirt and grime
Can be washed away leaving a shine.
I love the tuna that comes in brine
I don't like fresh fish with all that slime
I love the aroma of the pine
I love the milk shake that
Is flavored with lime
I like to see washing hanging on the line
Because it means that the weather is fine
I saw this lad he was about nine
Over some rocks he would bravely climb
To know a person who in their prime
Neglects themselves, it is such a crime.

And to hear a person really whine
Shouting 'you can't have it, because it's mine!'
So here I am at the end of this rhyme
Thanx for your attention and your time

My Two White Mice

One special day that was really nice
I was allowed to keep two white mice

I had heard about these mice
That their owner did not want.
They were kept in a box
With a window in the front.

I had to keep them in the cloakroom
High up on a shelf.
I had to feed them and clean their box,
And, keep them safe, all by myself.

You see I was living in a cottage away from home
And although with other children I still felt alone.

I would take care of my mice, every day
And would even let them out to have a play.
One sunny day I put the box on the green
In front of the cottage where I could be seen.

With my mice in my hands
And sitting under a tree
Some children had gathered
To watch the mice and me.

I was really glad when I was told
That I would not leave my pets behind
Mum had said I could take them home
Because really, she did not mind.

Having my mice felt like pure rapture
But I will leave the story for another chapter....

Dedicated to my mum

My mum could knit
She could do fair isle
Her needles would click
For quite a while

A jumper a pullover
Or a cardigan
Was often knitted
For a man or a woman

For us she would knit
Gloves and socks
She even knitted
Pretty warm frocks

Some would have bobbles
Some had cable
To follow any pattern
Mum was well able

Scotty dogs and rabbits
For the boys to wear
Chicks and teddies
For the girls were fair

Turtle neck, V neck
Raglan sleeves too
There would always be patterns
Old and new

I could never knit as good as her
To me she was the best
No more winding of the wool
Because she is now at rest.

Never Again!

The time came for the annual trip
To the Lake District in our car
We would stay in the caravan for the week
Where the walk to the pub was not far
My late husband was a keen fisherman
He would fish on the river for trout
I would often be left 'bored' in the van
His fishing meant he was off 'out'

The day before we were leaving
He suggested I give it a try
He took me to a cottage
Where the river was close by
He parked the car and from the boot
He handed me some waders
The sight of me now? just imagine
Have you ever seen 'The Invaders'

I struggled down to the river
With a fly rod in my hand
I was placed in the shallow water
Hoping, a trout I would land
I stood there for what seemed like hours
Before my hubby came back
He watched me for a little while
Smiled, saying "I had the knack"

By now the moon was shining
And I had not caught a fish
"Come here, he said he knew a place
Where I just could not miss"
We followed a path and met a style
And with waders up to my chest
I must have looked quite clumsy
But still I did my best.

We plodded on 'til a gap appeared
Among the many trees
Here it is, its not too deep....
Just above the knees.
Well I stepped in feeling afraid
Of slipping in this river
The water now above my waist
I began to shiver.

I made sure that I felt steady
As I began to cast
Just how long will I be standing here
But WOW a fish at last!
But I could not see a thing
The reel it kept on spinning
I raised my hand with the moon behind
But I could not stop the fish from swimming

"Where are you"! I screamed aloud
As the fish, it got away
Then in the darkness the silhouette
Of my hubby "I'm here" I heard him say.
Just then I felt an eel slither round my leg
And now I was so angry as I felt he let me down
You should not have put me here, then go and leave me to it
What would you do if I had slipped "leave me to drown?"!

I slowly waded towards him, there on the bank
As he helped me, up the slippy slope
In future I will stay in the van
It is boring but I will cope
So never again will I try to fish
I'll stick to cooking them instead
I don't even like trout
Alive or even dead!

YUK!

Dear Mr Sunshine

Well we hoped for blooms in May
Here it is June already
With just one bright day of sunshine
"We must really take it steady"!

We will see what "Flaming June" will bring
I'm prepared with "factor 8"
I don't use the sun beds
I'll get no tan at this rate

Not like my sister, she is tanned all year
She goes abroad to the sun
She will use the sun bed with no fear
And seems to have such fun.

So, Mr sunshine we are here for you
Make us all happy please
We need the sky of blue!!

Give the clouds a rest
Make them go away
And let us have some sunshine TODAY!

I Love the Peony

I so love the Peony when in full bloom
But they are so heavy they need plenty of room
I pick them up when they fall to the ground
Just three in a vase is plenty I've found.
I have some pale pink ones in the window today
I really love the Peony in every way.

I have placed one in an ash tray all on its own
For me to admire right next to the phone
I cannot believe that in my garden they grew
They look so majestic and healthy too.
I count my blessings thanking God each day
And with blooms like this, what can I say
Such beautiful flowers at their best
Yes dear Lord I am truly Blessed

The Dandelion

In many gardens all around
About this time of year
The maintenance is very hard
As many weeds now appear

The children now make daisy chains
The little daisy is so sweet
But alas the dreaded Dandelion
Grows everywhere in the street.

It is a shame that the Dandelion
Is classed as such a weed
They can form a yellow carpet
Until they go to seed.

No one is safe from them
They spread like a disease
And when in the flower bed
They bring us to our knees

To kill this yellow flower
Does not seem very fair
But armed with my weed killer
I really do not care

There really is no place for it
In neat gardens of today
So, sorry to the Dandelion
But please, just GO AWAY!

Wednesday and it is "HOT"

Well here we are its "Wednesday"
And boy it is hot!
We've been asking for sunshine
And this is what we got!
No need for the sun bed––rather the shade
Not under the trees, not safe I'm afraid
Up with the parasol down with the blinds
So hot in the cars and buses one finds
Drinks of bottled water, a dip in the pool
Loads of ice cream trying to keep cool
The heart of summer now in July
The heat is now with us—doesn't time fly
Trying with the fan to give cool air
But even 'that' is warm no matter where

Even the nights are humid and heavy
So unpleasant we know
I for one don't know what's worse
The blazing sun or freezing snow!
"Stay cool" is what I say...
PHEW!

Well again it's Wednesday

Well it's another Wednesday
No two are the same
Last week was sunshine
This week it's rain.

But then as we meet
This jolly afternoon
We'll forget about the rain
There maybe sunshine soon.

So now despite the weather
We are here to have some fun
Programmes we have each week
Must be enjoyed by everyone

So give a wave to each other
Let them know you're here
To share the afternoon with them
Should they ever fear.

But being in this little church
And in this community
We can safely say, like today
This is the place to be.
'It's a piece of cake'

My new gadget the Wii

Here I am aged 66
Having purchased 'a WII'
I am trying out some new tricks
Much to the surprise of my family
I've been told to exercise, painful I know
Never the less I will give it go

Trouble is my body is tense
And also very stiff
I just know that I will sweat
creating Quite a wiff
This should not be a problem
Since I live alone
I must try to loosen up
Give my muscles 'tone'

Well today's the day, I've set up the Wii
And on my swivel chair, I will sit
I want to play bowls and taking it slow
'Cos I'm sure that my body's unfit
Well here I go, what the heck
At least it's a game that I know
"Nice strike! Nice spare!
I'm so excited, just watch me go!

By now I'm on my feet
Now looking to try some golf
This should be great fun
As a beginner I'll use my loaf
Now let me see, oh I must practice first
With the gadget in my hand
Well here goes I give it a swing
Not sure where the ball will land
I know that I must not give up
but on the green the game is tough
So many times I've missed the ball
Maybe my swing is not good enough

'Oh deary me' I have just checked
To see what I'm doing wrong
Maybe its the 'wrong' button
I've been pressing all along
But then with more practice
I have completed the nine holes
But now that I'm exhausted
I will return to playing bowls

Well it has been over an hour
I must now have a rest
I will try again tomorrow
And put my fitness to the test
Next day has now arrived
And the pain in my back is sore
I will leave it for another day
'cos I am not ready for any more
It was great fun and I'll use it again
I want to get fit somehow
I must really expect some pain
'But it is back in the box for now.'

My time in the Market

Today in the covered market
I went to look around
When suddenly some people stood
Where a lady lay on the ground
This lady had stumbled and was hurt
And a first aider was on the scene
With help this lady was then propped up
Against a stall where she could lean
In no time at all a medic arrived
With a chair for the lady to sit
When this poor lady now in shock
Was having some kind of fit
Some of the people had moved away
To give the poor lady some air
Once the lady had recovered enough
She was taken outside on the chair
There an Ambulance was waiting
And the lady was soon inside
I admired the care that was taken
I dread to think 'if that lady had died'

Once the drama was over
And I could focus again
I found what I was looking for
On the stall in the middle lane
Then once I had got my purchase
I took out my mobile phone
I rang for my usual taxi
And in no time at all I was home.
"What a day"

The Military Tattoo

Such enthusiasm, and really I am sure
That being so positive makes it even more
Fun when at the rendezvous, meeting you today
Watching birds overhead, chirping as they play.
Going to the battle field to watch the show
And admiring the armour that they own, you know.
There is also a showing of the odd parachute
Then of all the forces and their fine salute.
We see some children slide, like slipping on soap
Speeding down with a scream on a guided rope
We have seen the beefeaters with their long red coats
And loads of happy people, on their colourful floats.
There has been loud music with the military band
They were looking so professional on the band stand
The smell from the NAFFI tent wets the appetite
With all of the fresh food tender to the bite.
It really is delicious we really want to stay
But then the next event lures us both away

We watched as the sailors build up rigging oh so high,
Then when the sailors climb it, we begin to wonder why?
But then, to the music and in perfect synchronization
The sailors show was faultless during all of their formation.
There is a cheer in this arena,
The finale does not lack
All of the excitement and we're glad to have come back.
There's last announcement is now follow my lead
As the day is now over, its been very good indeed.
The lovely song has shown and with laughter all around

We all heading for the gate and now leave the ground
We're all happy to leave with our farewells said
Heading for the comfort of our homes and bed.
End.

The Pen

I remember at school when learning to write
I began with a pencil with an end I would bite.
My feelings were hurt when the teacher would view
That my writing was awful and my spelling too.
But worse to come, how I remember the day
When introduced to the inkwells, that were on a tray.

There was a pencil with a funny looking end
"That's where the nib goes" said my friend.
I looked in dismay as I took hold of this pen
I felt the sharp nib, saying "what now then"?

I dipped it in the inkwell and saw the ink load
Take off the access, write your name I'm told.
We also had blotting paper all nice and clean
But to put pen to paper, I was not very keen.

As I touched the paper, a blot would appear
I got very nervous as my teacher came near
"What have we here" when she saw the blot
I blushed bright red and became very hot.

I tried again with this new Idea
But the nib "split", adding to my fear.
The blotting paper by now, was almost full
From the splashes and the blot's "tut, oh wonderful"!

I'd create a picture from these blots of mine
Hoping I'd get used to that nib, given time.
I later had a "fountain pen" a fine one indeed
Ink flowed on its own whenever the need.

I still used the pencil now and then
Better for drawing, than any pen.

But then the day came "what a revolution"
The "biro" was now in use, in every institution.
This "biro pen" what a blessing, it's true
Really great, in red, black, green and blue.
Useful in café's in village, city, town
All over the place for "writing orders down".

Now advanced to the marker pen, felt tip pens galore
With every colour thought about and sometimes even more.
The nibs are very different in size and even shape
And the need for these pens, I just cannot escape.

I have come a long way since the "inkwell".....
And 'tho still rather rough....
And at least I can write and spell
And to me "that's good enough".
Thank you.

Printed and bound by CPI Group (UK) Ltd, Croydon, CR0 4YY